WORDS OF INSPIRATION TO ENCOURAGE YOUR DAILY Journey

MINNIE WALKER-SIMMONS, PHD

authorHOUSE®

AuthorHouse™
1663 Liberty Drive
Bloomington, IN 47403
www.authorhouse.com
Phone: 1 (800) 839-8640

Published by AuthorHouse   12/29/2016

ISBN: 978-1-5246-5528-0 (sc)
ISBN: 978-1-5246-5527-3 (e)

Library of Congress Control Number: 2016920716

Print information available on the last page.

Acknowledgement

Throughout my life God endowed me with a gift of writing and has inspired me over the years with various inspirational quotations, poems, and short stories.

I am immensely grateful to God from the depths of my heart and soul to be specifically selected and entrusted with this gift to share with others.

Next, I want to thank my mother, Mable Walker, who has journeyed on to be present with the Lord, for building a foundation by being a strong role model for me. A widow, supportive, understanding woman while I was yet in search of my earthly, spiritual purpose in life. I feel that her spirit is pleased and proud of my relationship with God and my acceptance of HIS call.

Heartfelt thanks to my spouse, Dennis, who encourages, prays, and supports me in any aspects of my ministry. What more can you ask for from a spouse?

To all my children, Miguel, Sherrell, Terry, and Tezzie that understands now, my absence in their early childhood equated to attending college plus working to make a financial foundation for them as a single parent. I pray that each will find their own life purpose and accepts God's call.

Last, but not least, to my brother, Jesse, that made a caring choice when I was growing up, to forfeit a college education and remain home in order to support our mother and myself. What a sacrifice! This decision has touched my heart and my inner being, which has given me remarkable undying respect for him. May God bless his latter years and add to his days.

Introduction

Life sometimes throws a fast, curve ball in our direction that may cause us to strike occasionally, but not to strike out.

I hope these inspirational quotations will fill your heart, mind, soul, spirit with joy, and peace endowing you with strength to home run your struggles and challenges out of the park.

Enjoy and be richly blessed.

"STAY ON THE WALL AND DON'T COME DOWN."

(My Pastor, Overseer, Prophetess, Dorothy Craft)

"LET MY WISH BE FULFILLED"

"LET MY WORDS BE HARKENED UNTO"

"LET MY PRAYERS BE RECEIVED"

"IN JESUS NAME".

(The Late Founder, Prophetess, Pastor Amber Jean Barber)

INSPIRATIONAL QUOTATIONS FOR DAILY LIFE CHALLENGES

MINNIE W. SIMMONS, PhD

"The darkness will disappear in your life when you discover there is light after you open your eyes."

And God said, "let there be light."

"If you love nature, you have respect for God's creation."

God created the heavens and the earth and everything in them was good.

"As you travel the road of life, beware of the many detours that you will encounter.

Walk in the way of good men, and keep the paths of the righteous.

The quieter that one's becomes, the better they can hear and understand what is being said."

Incline thine ear unto wisdom, and apply thine heart to understanding.

"Live today as if the clock is on the count down to 1 in 10 seconds."

No man knows the hour for the end of their life on earth.

"Life is your interpretation of what is happening around you."

For the lord giveth wisdom; out of his mouth cometh knowledge and understanding.

"If you could see tomorrow, there would be no need for what tomorrow will bring."

New life and new mercies are gifts for each tomorrow.

"Tomorrow is the beginning of yesterday."

For a thousand years in thy sight are but as yesterday
when it is past, and as a watch in the night.

"Challenges are unconquered nightmares."

There is nothing too hard for God to conquer.

"God is, God was, God will forever be God."

God will never change. He is omnipotent,
omnipresent, and omniscience.

"Beauty is in the eyes of all those that appreciate God's creation."

Consider thy heavens, and the work of thy fingers, the moon and the stars, which thou hast ordained.

"Youth is a sense of carelessness and carefree."

Happy is the man that findeth wisdom, and the man that getteth understanding.

"A dream is an incomplete idea."

Ask and you shall receive. Knock and the door will swing open.

"Give a gift of prayer to everyone, the cost is free."

Prayer is a powerful weapon.

"You can always email God; he does not use spam blocker."

God is an infinite God.

"If you desire to make changes in your life, the first step is to conquer your fears."

Be not afraid of fear, neither of the desolation of the wicked, when it cometh. For the Lord shall be thy confidence.

"Fear impedes all progress."

Trust in God and thou shalt walk in thy way safely,
and thy foot shall not stumble.

"Judge no one until you have sat in front of a jury."

Judge ye not. Our heavenly father is the supreme judge.

"A healthy personality attracts a healthy acquaintance."

Turn not to the right hand nor to the left: remove thy foot from evil.

"Measure the company you keep by the progress you make."

Go from the presence of a foolish man, when thou perceivest not in him the lips of knowledge.

"Turn off the noise. What do you hear?"

A wise man will hear, and will increase learning; and a man of understanding shall attain unto wise counsels.

"Shhh! What is your inner being saying?"

Put away from thee a forward mouth, and perverse
lips put far from thee.

"Concentrate on the good in your life, then the bad will be eliminated."

Let thine heart retain God's words; keep his commandments and live.

"To adopt a good habit, repeat it five consecutive times".

A wise man is strong; yea, a man of knowledge increaseth strength.

"Positive thoughts=Positive actions.

As a man thinketh, so is he.

"Change your thoughts and you can change your destiny."

I have taught thee in the way of wisdom; I have led thee in the right paths.

"You can rate yourself the number one original and there will not be a need to imitate anyone.'

For thou hast made man a little lower than God, and crowned him with glory and honor.

"Uplift someone's heart and spirit today by saying I LOVE YOU and I believe in you."

With loving kindness, I have drawn thee.

"The greatest use of life is to share it with someone that embraces the same goals and ideas."

Behold, I belong to God like you; I too have been formed out of the clay.

"All that glitters is not genuine."

The lip of truth shall be established forever; but a
lying tongue is but for a moment.

"Show an act+ of kindness today, tomorrow may be too late."

Be kind to one another, tender-hearted, forgiving each other, just as God in Christ also has forgiven you.

"Wisdom starts with knowing when to open your mouth and when to keep it closed."

The fear of the lord is the beginning of knowledge; but fools despise wisdom and instructions.

"If you fall today, don't wait until tomorrow to get up."

For a righteous man falls seven times, and rises again, But the wicked stumble in time of calamity.

"Wisdom is appreciating the beginning of each day."

Know that wisdom is thus for your soul; If you find
it, then there will be a future, and your hope will not
be cut off.

"Life is, life was, life will always be life as long as you are breathing."

As for man, his days are like grass; As a flower of the field, so he flourishes. When the wind has passed over it, it is no more, And its place acknowledges it no longer.

"Don't rush tomorrow for it will come soon enough."

So do not worry about tomorrow; for tomorrow will care for itself. Each day has enough trouble of its own.

"Be careful how you interact and treat an individual, that person may be your boss tomorrow."

"But love your enemies, and do good, and lend, expecting nothing in return; and your reward will be great, and you will be sons of the Most High; for He Himself is kind to ungrateful and evil men.

"Life treats us sometimes like a glass of unsweetened tea; add a little artificial sweetener and drink up."

Many are the afflictions of the righteous, But the LORD delivers him out of them all.

"Take back control of your life today; forgive someone that has hurt you in the past."

Whenever you stand praying, forgive, if you have anything against anyone, so that your Father who is in heaven will also forgive you your transgressions.

"Academic knowledge is what you paid for to acquire; wisdom is what you earned free from experience."

Take my instruction and not silver, And knowledge rather than choicest gold. For wisdom is better than jewels; And all desirable things cannot compare with her.

"Opportunity is knocking at your door, remove the deadbolt lock and allow it to come in."

We must work the works of Him who sent Me as long as it is day; night is coming when no one can work.

"If you fall down in the race; crawl to the finish line."

For we all stumble in many ways If anyone does not stumble in what he says, he is a perfect man, able to bridle the whole body as well.

"Spoken words are powerful; so think carefully
before you open your mouth."

Let the words of my mouth and the meditation of my
heart Be acceptable in Your sight, O LORD, my Rock
and my Redeemer.

"Once words leave your mouth, they will not turn around and return before they reach their destination."

My mouth is filled with Your Praise and with Your glory all day long.

"Smile today at someone, you'll reduce the number of wrinkles."

Beloved, if God so loved us, we also ought to love one another.

"When you are angry keep your mouth closed and listen to what your heart is saying."

Let all bitterness and wrath and anger and clamor and slander be put away from you, along with all malice.

"Happiness is maintaining a positive attitude toward life."

You will make known to me the path of life; In Your presence is fullness of joy; In Your right hand there are pleasures forever.

"Happiness is sharing and caring life with someone that is special."

Where there is no vision, the people are unrestrained, but happy is he who keeps the law.

"Diffuse your angry energy with relaxation."

Let all bitterness and wrath and anger and clamor
and slander be put away from you, along with all
malice.

"Love yourself; give you a big hug daily."

Do you not know that you are a temple of God and
that the Spirit of God dwells in you? If any man
destroys the temple of God, God will destroy him, for
the temple of God is holy, and that is what you are.

"To live peaceful is to keep a clear conscious."

And the peace of God, which surpasses all comprehension, will guard your hearts and your minds in Christ Jesus.

"Don't compare your weakness with others strengths."

He gives strength to the weary, and to him who lacks might He increases power. Yet those who wait for the LORD Will gain new strength.

"Never let the day end without saying at least one complimentary thing to your life's companion."

Let all bitterness and wrath and anger and clamor and slander be put away from you, along with all malice. Be kind to one another, tender-hearted, forgiving each other, just as God in Christ also has forgiven you.

"Neglect the whole world rather than yourself."

Know that your body is God's temple, not your own.

"Married companions should never yell at each other unless the house is on fire."

Nevertheless, each individual among you also is to love his own wife even as himself, and the wife must see to it that she respects her husband.

"Wisdom is seeking advice from others."

But if any of you lacks wisdom, let him ask of God,
who gives to all generously and without reproach,
and it will be given to him.

"Wisdom is accepting the fact that you have room for growth."

For I will give you utterance and wisdom which none of your opponents will be able to resist or refute.

"Understand the others point of view; you may learn something new."

He who despises his neighbor lacks sense, but a man of understanding keeps silent.

"Let go of emotional debt, it keeps you trapped in the past and your account with a past due balance."

And forgive us our debts, as we also have forgiven our debtors.

"Light a candle today to wipe out the darkness in your heart."

Then Jesus again spoke to them, saying, "I am the Light of the world; he who follows Me will not walk in the darkness, but will have the Light of life."

"Laugh, it will reduce gloom."

Blessed are you who hunger now, for you shall be satisfied. Blessed are you who weep now, for you shall laugh.

"Give someone a gentle hug to show them that somebody cares."

Beloved, if God so loved us, we also ought to love one another.

"Knowledge is a lifetime investment."

A wise man is strong, And a man of knowledge
increases power.

"Laughter is a non-prescriptive medicine."

Even in laughter the heart may be in pain, And the end of joy may be grief.

"You can become an excellent leader after you have learned to become a humble follower."

"Whoever exalts himself shall be humbled; and whoever humbles himself shall be exalted.

"A true friend is someone that values you, never judges you, offers support, forgives your mistakes, and raises your spirits."

A friend loves at all times, and a brother is born for adversity.

"Wisdom is acknowledging that you don't know everything and has an open mind to accept corrections with a smile and thank you."

Make your ear attentive to wisdom, incline your heart to understanding; For if you cry for discernment, lift your voice for understanding.

"A hug a day keeps depression away; if you need a hug ask for it."

Since you have in obedience to the truth purified your souls for a sincere love of the brethren, fervently love one another from the heart.

"Shedding tears releases pressure from our emotional thermometer."

"Hear my prayer, O LORD, and give ear to my cry; Do not be silent at my tears; For I am a stranger with You, A sojourner like all my fathers.

"Be careful with the flowers you pick; you may end up with a poisonousness blossom."

As for man, his days are like grass; As a flower of the field, so he flourishes. When the wind has passed over it, it is no more, and its place acknowledges it no longer.

"Hope is an anchor that keeps our soul from sinking."

For You are my hope; O Lord GOD, You are my confidence from my youth.

"We gain victory in our lives over negative situations when our thoughts line up with God's word".

But prove yourselves doers of the word, and not merely hearers who delude themselves. For if anyone is a hearer of the word and not a doer, he is like a man who looks at his natural face in a mirror.

"Your actions result from your thoughts."

Therefore, do my thoughts cause me to answer, and
for this I make haste.

"Happiness penetrates, overflows from the inside to the outside."

O the happiness of a man who hath found wisdom,
and of a man who bringeth forth understanding.

"When you send love out to someone, a boomerang will return with the same."

Beloved, let us love one another, for love is from God; and everyone who loves is born of God and knows God.

"Give love and feel happiness."

A new commandment I give to you, that you love one another, even as I have loved you, that you also love one another.

"Each day of your life should be better than the day before."

When I was a child, I used to speak like a child, think like a child, reason like a child; when I became a man, I did away with childish things.

"Sprinkle a little spice in your life daily to give it a little zest."

O LORD, be gracious to us; we have waited for You
Be their strength every morning, Our salvation also
in the time of distress.

"Remember what you say, what you do, what you are thinking –somebody is watching and listening."

The eyes of the LORD are in every place, Watching
the evil and the good.

"Be the leader of your life-don't give someone else the reins."

Remember those who led you, who spoke the word of God to you; and considering the result of their conduct, imitate their faith.

"What we believe can affect our progress in life."

Truly, truly, I say to you, he who believes in Me, the
works that I do, he will do also; and greater works
than these he will do; because I go to the Father.

"Change our belief and we can change our thinking."

And Jesus said to him, "'If You can?' All things are possible to him who believes."

"Who you want to be and what you want to become is within your own God given power."

You see that a man is justified by works and not by faith alone.

"Look for the message when trouble comes your way."

Call upon Me in the day of trouble; I shall rescue you, and you will honor Me.

"Give thanks to the miniature things, for tomorrow it will become gigantic."

"He who offers a sacrifice of thanksgiving honors Me; And to him who orders his way aright I shall show the salvation of God."

"If you fail, change your direction and go another way."

There is no failure in God. Trust in Him for directions.

"Hope is a flotation device that keeps a head above the water."

And now, Lord, what wait I for? my hope *is* in thee.

"We gain victory in our lives over negative situations when our thoughts lineup with positive thinking."

"Finally, brothers and sisters, whatever is true, whatever is noble, whatever is right, whatever is pure, whatever is lovely, whatever is admirable–if anything is excellent or praiseworthy–think about such things."

"We cannot get to our next stage in life until we make a start."

Therefore, my beloved brethren, be steadfast, immovable, always abounding in the work of the Lord, knowing that your toil is not in vain in the Lord.

"Think about what you are thinking about."

The plans of the mind and orderly thinking belong to man, but from the Lord comes the wise answer of the tongue.

"Your actions are the results of your thoughts."

For I have known the thoughts that I
am thinking towards you -- an affirmation of
Jehovah; thoughts of peace, and not of evil, to give to
your posterity and hope.

"Give yourself permission to be successful."

The Lord grants success to the one whose behavior
he finds commendable.

"Your tongue is a magnet that can draw positive or negative things."

Teach me, and I will hold my tongue and cause me to understand wherein I have erred.

"Put on a fresh new attitude daily."

God, create a pure heart in me, and renew a
right attitude within me.

"Sew a seed of love today by giving someone a big gentle hug."

Hatred stirreth up strifes; but love covereth all sins.

"Give four powerful words of encouragement; you can do it"!

The craftsman encourages the metalworker; the one who flattens with the hammer supports the one who strikes the anvil, saying of the soldering, "It is good." He fastens it with nails so that it will not fall over.

"Life is like a puzzle; it will only be fulfilled if you collect the right pieces that fit."

Happy (blessed, fortunate, enviable) is the man who finds skillful and godly Wisdom, and the man who gets understanding [drawing it forth from God's Word and life's experiences],

"It's not what you ask for, it's how you phrase your words."

"Death and life are in the power of the tongue, and those who love it will eat its fruits."

"Align yourself in the right position to receive the blessings that are available."

He who is kind will have a blessing, for he gives of his bread to the poor.

"Give love and compassion and it will return on a silver platter."

But love ye your enemies, and do good, show compassion to them and lend, hoping for nothing again; and your reward shall be great, and ye shall be the children of the Highest.

"Respect yourself and others will pattern themselves
from observing you."

And the second *is* like, *namely* this, Thou shalt
love thy neighbour as thyself. There is none other
commandment greater than these.

"Forgiveness is a powerful weapon."

And become one to another kind, tender-hearted,
forgiving one another, according as also God in
Christ did forgive you.

"Joy is endless and eternal."

You will make known to me the path of life; In Your presence is fullness of joy; In Your right hand there are pleasures forever.

"Weeping may release lingering frustrations."

The Lamb in the center of the throne will be their
shepherd, and will guide them to springs of the
water of life; and God will wipe every tear from their
eyes."

"Healthy mind+ healthy heart+ healthy body
+healthy lifestyle=LONGEVITY!"

But you shall serve the LORD your God, and He will
bless your bread and your water; and I will remove
sickness from your midst.

"We all need someone else to survive. Living is not individualistic."

Two are better than one because they have a good return for their labor.

"When making a critical decision, don't follow your heart, use your head because that's where your brain is located."

But if any of you lacks wisdom, let him ask of God, who gives to all generously and without reproach, and it will be given to him.

"If you are dealt a bad hand from the deck, reshuffle
and try again."

The LORD is good, a stronghold in the day of trouble,
And He knows those who take refuge in Him.

"Life is full of beautiful flowers, which one will you pick?"

If you walk in My ways and keep My statutes and commandments just as your father David did, I will give you a long life.

"Hug someone today because they may not have any arms, so share yours."

Be devoted to one another in brotherly love; give preference to one another in honor.

"If you are tired of walking, exchange shoes with someone else."

If you have run with footmen and they have tired you out, then how can you compete with horses? If you fall down in a land of peace, how will you do in the thicket of the Jordan?

"Life is full of surprises; don't let it catch you off guard."

The thief comes only to steal and kill and destroy; I came that they may have life, and have it abundantly.

"Smile, it is a prevention treatment to keep wrinkles away."

For You, O LORD, have made me glad by what You have done, I will sing for joy at the works of Your hands.

"Spread a little cheer today; smile."

A joyful heart makes a cheerful face, But when the heart is sad, the spirit is broken.

"Be grateful for little things because many little things=Big things."

Oh give thanks to the LORD, for He is good, For His lovingkindness is everlasting.

"Decrease your overload before it throws you over the load."

And the peace of God, which surpasses all comprehension, will guard your hearts and your minds in Christ Jesus.

"Love is a beautiful emotion that is treasured until the earth stops rotating."

For God so loved the world, that He gave His only begotten Son, that whoever believes in Him shall not perish, but have eternal life.

"Reflect on the past to achieve a better future."

I do not regard myself as having laid hold of it yet;
but one thing I do: forgetting what lies behind and
reaching forward to what lies ahead, I press on
toward the goal for the prize of the upward call of
God in Christ Jesus.

"Love, Live, Laugh, and enjoy Life Lessons."

Keep my commandments and live, And my teaching
as the apple of your eye.

"Stand up for yourself, or you will remain stuck in your seat forever."

Put on the full armor of God, so that you will be able to stand firm against the schemes of the devil.

"Make plans for today and complete the list, for you may not reach tomorrow."

Boast not thyself of tomorrow; for thou knowest not what a day may bring forth.

"Explore something new today; for it will empower your knowledge."

A wise man is strong, And a man of knowledge increases power.

"Don't be afraid to make a mistake, it's part of our learning process."

For a righteous man falls seven times, and rises again, But the wicked stumble in time of calamity.

"Embrace your passion; take some time and do something you enjoy today."

And do not neglect doing good and sharing, for with such sacrifices God is pleased.

"Life is filled with many possibilities; which one will you pick?"

You who fear the LORD, trust in the LORD; He is their help and their shield.

"Strength is not how much weight you can lift, but how much weight that you can carry on your shoulders without falling to the ground."

He gives strength to the weary, and to him who lacks might He increases power.

"Your strength +weakness =Human.

Do not fear, for I am with you; Do not anxiously look
about you, for I am your God I will strengthen you,
surely I will help you, Surely I will uphold you with
My righteous right hand.'

"Reach for the stars in the universe, but keep your feet anchored to the ground."

For whatever is born of God overcomes the world; and this is the victory that has overcome the world-- our faith.

"Spoon feeding teaches us only how to open our mouths; we don't need a brain to do that."

You are from God, little children, and have overcome them; because greater is He who is in you than he who is in the world.

"Extend a helping hand to someone that has lost their fingers."

Give, and it will be given to you. They will pour into your lap a good measure--pressed down, shaken together, and running over.

"Learn to love thyself before you can share it with someone else."

And he answering said, Thou shalt love the Lord thy God with all thy heart, and with all thy soul, and with all thy strength, and with all thy mind; and thy neighbour as thyself.

"Appreciate life's good and bad situations: Good +Bad = Growth

Now unto him that is able to do exceeding abundantly above all that we ask or think, according to the power that worketh in us.

"You have the authority to judge only one person, YOURSELF!"

Test yourselves to see if you are in the faith; examine yourselves! Or do you not recognize this about yourselves, that Jesus Christ is in you--unless indeed you fail the test?

"Be careful how you treat your body, you're only leasing it; it maybe come costly if not treated with care."

Do you not know that you are a temple of God and that the Spirit of God dwells in you?

"Happiness is a result of your inner being."

O taste and see that the LORD is good; How blessed
is the man who takes refuge in Him!

"Your inner being is your outer being."

Therefore, my heart is glad and my glory
my inner self-rejoices; my body too shall rest and
confidently dwell in safety,

"As you carry old hurt/anger around, you will begin to smell of garbage; empty your pail."

And forgive us our debts, as we forgive our debtors.

"Past painful experiences are buried history, don't dig it up."

He healeth the broken in heart, and bindeth up their wounds.

"True forgiveness is a result of amnesia."

Say not, I will do so to him as he hath done to me: I
will render to the man according to his work.

"Experience is the best teacher only when a lesson is learned."

So shall the knowledge of wisdom be unto thy soul:
when thou hast found it, then there shall be a reward,
and thy expectation shall not be cut off.

"Treat others the way that you want to be treated; tomorrow that person may be the one to give you a glass of water."

But I say unto you which hear, Love your enemies, do good to them which hate you, Bless them that curse you, and pray for them which despitefully use you. And unto him that smiteth thee on the one cheek offer also the other; and him that taketh away thy cloke forbid not to take thy coat also.

"Mistakes are a common part of life, as long as they are not repeated."

For in many things we offend all. If any man offends not in word, the same is a perfect man, and able also to bridle the whole body.

"Laughter is the best holistic medicine."

A merry heart doeth good like a medicine: but a broken spirit drieth the bones.

MY YOUR STRENGTH EACH DAY
MULTIPLY AS YOU PRAY,
AS GOD GRANTS YOUR REQUEST
TO SERVE HIM AT YOUR BEST.

Printed in the United States
By Bookmasters